"This book will be a 'super' and 'simple' re[...]  from anxiety, depression, and other psy[...] two expert clinicians, it provides a conc[...] essential strategies and procedures of c[...] for changing how to respond to moods and life problems.

> —**Riccardo Dalle Grave, MD,** coauthor of the book, *Cognitive Behavior Therapy for Adolescents with Eating Disorders*

"In just 153 pages, McKay and colleagues masterfully untangle the core strategies of CBT responsible for its effectiveness in alleviating emotional distress. Written in an easy, conversational manner, *Super Simple CBT* is packed with practical advice, skills-based exercises, and case examples that cut through the noise and detailed presentations found in many CBT workbooks. This primer is an excellent starting point if you're new to CBT or need greater clarity about this treatment approach."

> —**David A. Clark, PhD,** author of *The Anxious Thoughts Workbook* and *The Negative Thoughts Workbook*

"This super simple CBT book is based on the basic principles of CBT: that thoughts cause feelings, and we can change our feelings by changing our thoughts. Starting from that, the authors describe certain kinds of dysfunctional thinking, help the reader identify and respond to them, and provide useful and simple techniques like worry control and relaxation to help consolidate new patterns of thinking and feeling. This little book is not only on super simple CBT skills, but also on super effective skills for anxiety and low mood."

> —**Gregoris Simos, MD, PhD,** professor of psychopathology at the University of Macedonia in Greece

"*Super Simple CBT* provides an easy-to-read, focused overview of key CBT skills. You will learn how to identify thoughts that are related to your emotional distress, and how to develop more balanced and helpful thinking patterns. You will also learn practical skills to help you lead a happier and better life. The book is full of examples as well as helpful exercises and strategies. This is a book that could change your life."

—**Nina Josefowitz, PhD,** coauthor of *CBT Made Simple*

"CBT is the gold-standard way to help you think clearly, feel better, and act effectively. *Super Simple CBT* is like an easy-to-read cookbook with a scientifically tested recipe to overcome miseries and thrive. The authors splendidly show how you can take charge of your life. Use the ideas and exercises to free yourself from anxiety, depression, anger, and other painful emotions. You'll be glad you did."

—**Bill Knaus, EdD,** author of *The Cognitive Behavioral Workbook for Depression, The Cognitive Behavioral Workbook for Anxiety,* and *The Procrastination Workbook*

"*Super Simple CBT* is a super book. McKay, Davis, and Fanning have produced a much-needed text for anyone who is looking for a clear, accessible, and succinct introduction to CBT. I highly recommend it. It's simply brilliant."

—**Stefan G. Hofmann, PhD,** coauthor of *Learning Process-Based Therapy*

"I highly recommend *Super Simple CBT* to anyone who is struggling with worry, anxiety, or depression and is unsure about how to manage it. The authors have done an excellent job of presenting a comprehensive and research-based toolbox of CBT skills in a straightforward, approachable, and user-friendly manner."

—**Melisa Robichaud, PhD,** coauthor of *The Generalized Anxiety Disorder Workbook* and *The Worry Workbook*

"If you are looking for immediate, actionable steps to address your anxiety or depression, *Super Simple CBT* is a great place to start. The authors have expertly distilled the active ingredients of CBT into a straightforward, easy-to-read guide with linked worksheets that encourage daily practice without being overwhelming."

—**Jamie Micco, PhD, ABPP,** author of *The Worry Workbook for Teens*

Super Simple

CBT

6 Skills to Improve Your Mood in Minutes

—

MATTHEW McKAY, PHD
MARTHA DAVIS, PHD
PATRICK FANNING

New Harbinger Publications, Inc.

Publisher's Note

Distributed in Canada by Raincoast Books

NEW HARBINGER PUBLICATIONS is a registered trademark of New Harbinger Publications, Inc.

Copyright © 2022 by Matthew McKay, Patrick Fanning, and Martha Davis
New Harbinger Publications, Inc.
5674 Shattuck Avenue
Oakland, CA 94609
www.newharbinger.com

Cover design by Amy Shoup; Interior design by Amy Shoup and Michele Waters-Kermes; Acquired by Elizabeth Hollis Hansen

---

Library of Congress Cataloging-in-Publication Data

Names: McKay, Matthew, author. | Davis, Martha, author. | Fanning, Patrick, author.
Title: Super simple CBT : six skills to improve your mood in minutes / Matthew McKay, Martha Davis, Patrick Fanning.
Description: Oakland, CA : New Harbinger Publications, 2022. | Includes bibliographical references.
Identifiers: LCCN 2021037340 | ISBN 9781684038695 (trade paperback)
Subjects: LCSH: Cognitive therapy--Popular works.
Classification: LCC RC489.C63 M338 2022 | DDC 616.89/1425--dc23
LC record available at https://lccn.loc.gov/2021037340

Printed in the United States of America

24   23   22

10   9   8   7   6   5   4   3   2   1   First Printing

CONTENTS

INTRODUCTION

Life is hard. To cope, all of us have been given a random set of tools and instructions by parents, family, friends, teachers, bosses, and others. Some of this has been helpful, some not. This book gives you tools from cognitive behavioral therapy (CBT) that work. It is a guide for changing how you respond to your moods and your life.

You may believe painful feelings are caused by forgotten childhood experiences. Maybe you assume the only way to relieve these feelings is through long, difficult analysis to root out unconscious memories and associations.

There is some connection between your distant past and painful feelings in the present. But there is a much more immediate and accessible source of emotions: your current train of thought.

Two simple insights form the heart of CBT. The first is this:

1. Thoughts cause feelings.

Most emotions are immediately preceded by some kind of interpreting thought. For example, say a friend doesn't call when they said they would.

> If you think, "He doesn't like me after all," you might feel sadness or shame.

> If you think, "They must have been in an accident," you might feel fear and anxiety.

> If you think "She lied to me. She's blowing me off!" you might feel angry.

Different thoughts about the same event spark very different emotions. But there's something you may have noticed, reading this example. That something is expressed by the second simple insight at the heart of CBT:

2. You can change your feelings by changing your thoughts.

In any situation where thoughts are triggering emotional distress, cognitive behavioral tools can help. This is especially true for automatic or habitual thoughts.

Over the past sixty years, CBT researchers and therapists have created and road-tested tools based on these insights. They are practical, easy to learn, and can give relief—especially from anxiety and depression.

ANXIETY becomes a problem when you worry more days than not for at least six months. It is difficult to control and you likely experience these symptoms:

- restlessness
- fatigue
- difficulty concentrating
- irritability
- muscle tension
- sleep disturbance

DEPRESSION is when your mood is sad and nothing seems interesting or pleasurable. It can affect you through:

- your appetite, causing you to lose or gain weight

- sleeping a lot more or less than usual

- feeling restless and yet tired at the same time

- struggling to concentrate or make decisions, especially the decision to get up and do something

- feeling worthless

- a sense of hopelessness about life

If depression has you thinking seriously about suicide, this book is not enough. Please see a mental health professional as soon as possible.

CBT also helps with many other problems including:

- problematic anger

- perfectionism

- low self-esteem

- shame

- guilt

- procrastination

—

This little book teaches core tools and practices of CBT that you can start using to get relief from emotional suffering.

The first three chapters help you identify three kinds of thoughts that can become patterns and cause emotional suffering:

- automatic thoughts

- limited thinking

- hot thoughts

The next three chapters teach practices you can use to release old patterns of thinking and feeling, and learn new ones:

- relaxation (helpful for most issues)

- worry control (especially helpful for anxiety)

- mobilization (especially helpful for depression)

There are downloadable and printable materials available to support your super-simple CBT practices at http://www.newharbinger.com/48695. You are also welcome to use a journal instead. For a list of materials that provide additional support, see the Resources section at the end of this book.

—

Congratulations on embarking on this voyage of self-discovery and healing! The techniques presented in this book offer you real promise that help is on the way. With patience and a little effort, you can start to feel better soon.

Chapter 1

AUTOMATIC THOUGHTS

As you now know, thoughts cause feelings. Many emotions are preceded and caused by a thought, however abbreviated, fleeting, or unnoticed that thought may be.

This is often represented as the ABC model of emotions, where A stands for "activating event," B stands for "belief," or thought, and C stands for "consequence," or feeling:

(A) Event ➔ (B) Thought ➔ (C) Feeling

Here's an example:

A. EVENT: You get into your car and turn the key, and nothing happens.

B. THOUGHT: You interpret the event by saying to yourself, "Oh no! My battery's dead. This is awful! I'm stuck, and I'll be late."

C. FEELING: You experience an emotion appropriate to your thoughts. In this case, you feel depressed and anxious about being late.

But when you change the thought, you change the feeling.

If your next thought was, "My teenager must have left the car's lights on all night again," you might have felt anger. But if you had thought, "I'll have an extra cup of coffee, relax, and wait for a jump from the tow truck," you would have felt mild annoyance at most.

Automatic thoughts like these pop into your mind in response to a trigger and without your intent. In this chapter, you will learn how to recognize and uncover the automatic thoughts in this cycle. Then you will learn to hear your own automatic thoughts so you can begin to record them in a Thought Journal. This is an extremely useful approach for exploring, confronting, and changing patterns of negative thinking.

Feedback Loops

The event-thought-feeling sequence is the basic building block of emotional life. But the building blocks can become very jumbled and confusing. In real life, people typically don't experience a simple series of ABC reactions, each with its discrete activating event, thought, and resultant feeling. More often, a series of ABC reactions join to form a feedback loop in which the ending feeling from one sequence becomes the starting event for another sequence.

In the case of painful feelings, a negative feedback loop can occur. This happens when an uncomfortable feeling itself becomes an activating event: the subject of further thoughts, which produce more painful feelings, which become a larger event inspiring more negative thoughts, and so on.

Feelings have physiological components. When you experience emotions such as fear, anger, or joy, your heart speeds up, you breathe faster and less deeply, you sweat more, and blood vessels in different parts of your body contract or dilate.

Conversely, "quiet" emotions, such as depression, sadness, or grief, involve a slowing down of some of your physiological systems. Either way, both the emotion and the accompanying bodily sensations trigger an evaluation process in which you start trying to interpret and label what you feel.

Here's an example of a feedback loop.

If your car wouldn't start late at night when you were in a dangerous part of town, the negative feedback loop might go like this:

A. EVENT: Car doesn't start.

B. THOUGHT: "Oh no! This is awful. I'll be late—and this is a dangerous street."

C. FEELINGS: Heart beating fast, feeling hot and sweaty, irritation, anxiety.

B. THOUGHT: "I'm scared. I could get mugged—this is really bad!"

C. FEELINGS: Stomach clenching, hard to breathe, dizzy, fear.

B. THOUGHT: "I'm freaking out. I'll lose control. Can't move. Can't get safe."

C. FEELINGS: Strong adrenaline rush, panic.

As you can see, the loop can continue until you work yourself into a rage, anxiety attack, or deep depression.

Automatic Thoughts

You are constantly describing the world to yourself, giving each event or experience some label. You automatically make interpretations of everything you see, hear, touch, and feel. You judge events as good or bad, pleasurable or painful, safe or dangerous. This process colors all of your experiences, labeling them with private meanings.

These labels and judgments are fashioned from the unending dialogue you have with yourself, a waterfall of thoughts cascading down the back of your mind. These thoughts are constant and rarely noticed, but they are powerful enough to create your most intense emotions.

Automatic thoughts usually have the following characteristics, which we'll discuss in detail. They often:

- appear in shorthand.

- are believed.

- seem spontaneous.

- are "should," "ought," or "must."

- tend to "awfulize."

- are relatively idiosyncratic.

- are persistent and self-perpetuating.

- differ from the person's public statements.

- repeat certain themes.

- are learned.

Appear in Shorthand

Automatic thoughts often appear in shorthand, composed of just a few essential words phrased in telegraphic style: "lonely…getting sick…can't stand it…cancer…no good." One word or a short phrase functions as a label for a group of painful memories, fears, or self-reproaches.

An automatic thought needn't be expressed in words at all. It can be a brief visual image, an imagined sound or smell, or a physical sensation. For example, someone who was afraid of heights had a half-second image of the floor tilting and felt himself sliding down toward the window. This momentary fantasy triggered acute anxiety whenever he ascended above the third floor.

Sometimes an automatic thought is a brief reconstruction of an event in the past. For instance, a depressed person kept seeing the stairway in Macy's where her husband first announced his plan to leave her. The image of the stairway was enough to unleash all the feelings associated with that loss.

Occasionally an automatic thought can take the form of intuitive knowledge, without words, images, or sense impressions. For example, a chef who was plagued with self-doubt "just knew" that it was useless to try to get promoted to head chef.

Are Believed

Automatic thoughts typically seem very believable, no matter how illogical they appear upon analysis. For example, a man who reacted with rage to the death of his best friend actually believed for a time that his friend deliberately died to punish him.

Automatic thoughts have the same believable quality as direct sense impressions. You attach the same truth value to automatic thoughts as you do to sights and sounds in the real world. If you see people getting into a Porsche and have the thought "They're rich. They don't care about anyone but themselves," the judgment is as real to you as the color of the car.

Seem Spontaneous

You believe automatic thoughts because they are automatic. They seem to arise spontaneously out of ongoing events. They just pop into your mind, and you hardly notice them, let alone subject them to logical analysis.

Are "Should," "Ought," or "Must"

A woman whose husband had recently died thought, "You ought to go it alone. You shouldn't burden your friends." Each time the thought popped into her mind, she felt a wave of hopelessness. People torture themselves with shoulds, such as "I should be happy, more energetic, creative, responsible, loving, generous..." Each ironclad should precipitates a sense of guilt or a loss of self-esteem.

Shoulds are hard to eradicate, since their origin and function is actually adaptive. They are simple rules to live by that have worked in the past. They are templates for survival that you can access quickly in times of stress. The problem is that they become so automatic that you don't have time to analyze them, and so rigid that you can't modify them to fit changing situations.

Tend to Awfulize

Automatic thoughts predict catastrophe, see danger in everything, and always anticipate the worst. A stomachache is a symptom of cancer, or a look of distraction on a lover's face is the first sign of withdrawal. These catastrophic thoughts are the major source of anxiety.

Like shoulds, they are also hard to eradicate because of their adaptive function. They help you predict the future and prepare for the worst-case scenario.

Are Idiosyncratic

Here's an example of how different automatic thoughts can arise for different people in response to the same event. In a crowded theater, a woman suddenly stood up, slapped the face of the man next to her, and hurried up the aisle and out the exit. One woman who witnessed this event was frightened because she thought, "She's really going to get it when they get home." She imagined the details of a brutal beating and recalled times when she had been physically abused.

A teenager was angry because he thought, "That poor guy. He probably just wanted a kiss, and she humiliated him. What a bitch."

A middle-aged man, seeing his ex-wife's face set in angry lines, told himself, "Now he's lost her, and he'll never get her back," and felt depressed.

A social worker felt a sense of righteous pleasure as she thought, "Serves him right. I wish some of the timid women I know had seen that."

Each response was based on a unique way of viewing the stimulus event and resulted in a different strong emotion.

Are Persistent and Self-Perpetuating

Automatic thoughts are hard to turn off or change because they are reflexive and plausible. They weave unnoticed through the fabric of your internal dialogue and seem to come and go with a will of their own. One automatic thought tends to act as a cue for another and then another and another. You may have experienced this chaining effect as one depressing thought triggers a long chain of associated depressing thoughts.

Differ from Public Statements

Most people talk to others very differently from the way they talk to themselves. To others they usually describe events in their lives as logical sequences of cause and effect. But to themselves they may describe the same events with self-deprecating venom or dire predictions.

One executive calmly explained aloud, "Since I got laid off, I've been a little depressed." This matter-of-fact statement differed sharply from the actual thoughts that unemployment triggered in her: "I'm a failure. I'll never work again. My family will starve. I can't make it in this world." These thoughts left her with an image of spiraling down into a bottomless black pit.

Repeat Certain Themes

Chronic anger, anxiety, or depression results from a focus on one particular group of automatic thoughts to the exclusion of all contrary thoughts. The theme of anxious people is danger. You may be preoccupied with the anticipation of dangerous situations, forever scanning the horizon for future threats or pain. Depressed people often focus on the past and obsess on the theme of loss. You may also focus on your own failings and flaws. Chronically angry people repeat automatic thoughts about the seemingly deliberate hurtful behavior of others.

Preoccupation with these themes creates a kind of tunnel vision in which you think only one kind of thought and notice only one aspect of your environment, resulting in one predominant and usually quite painful emotion. Aaron Beck has used the term "selective abstraction" to describe this type of tunnel vision in which you look at one set of cues in your environment to the exclusion of all others.

Are Learned

Since childhood, people have been telling you what to think. You have been conditioned by family, friends, teachers, the media, and others to interpret events a certain way. Over the years, you have learned and practiced habitual patterns of automatic thoughts that are difficult to detect, let alone change. That's the bad news. The good news is, what has been learned can be unlearned and changed.

Listen to These Thoughts

Hearing your automatic thoughts is the first step in gaining control of unpleasant emotions. Most of your internal dialogue is harmless. The automatic thoughts that cause harm can be identified because they almost always precede a persistent painful feeling.

To identify the automatic thoughts that are causing an ongoing painful feeling, try to recall the thoughts you had just prior to the start of the emotion and those that go along with the sustained emotion. You can think of it as listening in on an intercom. The intercom is always on, even when you're conversing with others and going about your life. You are functioning in the world and are also talking to yourself at the same time.

Listen in on your internal dialogue and hear what you're telling yourself. Your automatic thoughts are assigning private, idiosyncratic meanings to many external events and internal sensations and making judgments and interpretations of your experience.

Automatic thoughts are often lightning fast and very difficult to catch. They flash on as a brief mental image or are telegraphed in a single word. Here are two methods for coping with the swiftness of these thoughts.

1. Reconstruct a problem situation.

Go over it again and again in your imagination until the painful emotion begins to emerge. What are you thinking as the emotion comes up? Regard your thoughts as a slow-motion film. Look at your internal dialogue frame by frame. Notice the millisecond it takes to say, "I can't stand it" or the half-second image of a terrifying event. Notice how you're internally describing and interpreting the actions of others: "She's bored." "He's putting me down."

2. Stretch out the shorthand.

Expand the shorthand statement into the original statement from which it was extracted. "Feeling sick" might stand for "I'm feeling sick and I know I'm going to get worse. I can't stand it." "Crazy" might mean "I feel like I'm losing control, and that must mean I'm going crazy. My friends will reject me." Hearing the shorthand isn't enough. It is necessary to identify with your entire interior argument in order to understand the distorted logic from which many painful emotions bloom.

Record the Thoughts

To appreciate the power of your automatic thoughts and the role they play in your emotional life, use a form to keep a Thought Journal. You can download one from http://www.newharbinger.com/48695 and print copies. Or you can use a notebook of your choosing.

As soon as possible after you experience an unpleasant feeling, record it. Then assess your distress level, using a scale of 0 to 100 in which 0 means the feeling causes no distress and 100 is the most distressing emotion you have ever felt.

Carry your Thought Journal with you at all times for at least one week, making an entry only when you feel a painful emotion. You may find that concentrating on your automatic thoughts makes the feelings worse for a while. Keep working on it—it's normal to feel worse before you start to feel better.

Counting Thoughts

Sometimes automatic thoughts come so quickly and in such abbreviated form that you can't identify them, even though you know you just had some. In that case, you can simply count your thoughts. Carry an index card with you, and each time you notice that you've had an automatic thought, make a mark on the card. You can also keep a count of your episodes of automatic thoughts on a golf wrist counter or a knitting stitch counter.

Counting your automatic thoughts will help you get some distance from them, as well as a feeling of control. Rather than assuming that your automatic thoughts are an accurate assessment of events, you can note them and let them go. Once you've counted a thought, you needn't dwell on it.

This process will eventually slow your thoughts and sharpen your attention so the content of the thoughts starts to become clear. When that happens, you may want to continue counting but also start categorizing your thoughts and counting how many you have of various types: catastrophic thoughts, thoughts about loss, insecure thoughts, and so on.

If you forget to count your thoughts, set your phone or watch alarm or a timer to go off every twenty minutes. When the alarm goes off, stop what you're doing, look inside yourself, and count any negative thoughts you notice.

—

The process of uncovering automatic thoughts may make you begin to distrust these thoughts and start questioning and disputing them as they pop up.

At this point, it's important for you to recognize that thoughts create and sustain emotions. To reduce the frequency of painful emotions, you need to listen to what you think, then ask how true your thoughts are. Remember, what you think ultimately creates what you feel.

Chapter 2

LIMITED
THINKING

Someone walks up to a drugstore counter and asks for a particular brand of dental floss. The clerk says it's out of stock. The person concludes that the clerk has the dental floss but just wants to get rid of him because she doesn't like his looks. This logic seems obviously irrational and paranoid.

But consider the case of a husband coming home with a cloudy look on his face. His wife immediately concludes that he's angry because she was too tired to make love the previous night. She expects to be hurt by some sort of retaliation and quickly responds by becoming peevish and defensive. This logic makes perfect sense to her, and she doesn't question her conclusion until she learns that her husband had a minor auto accident on the way home.

The progression of logic she used goes like this:

1. My husband looks upset.

2. My husband often gets upset when I disappoint him.

3. Therefore, he's upset with me for disappointing him.

The problem with this logic lies in her assumptions that her husband's moods always relate to her and that she is the prime cause of his ups and downs. This pattern of limited thinking, called personalization, is the tendency to relate all the objects and events around you to yourself. Personalization limits you and causes pain because you consistently misinterpret what you see and then act on that misinterpretation.

This chapter will examine eight limited thinking patterns and give you practice in identifying them. Then it will teach you to analyze the automatic thoughts in your Thought Journal, and identify which of the limited thinking patterns you habitually employ in difficult situations. You'll learn how to compose balanced alternative self-statements that will become more believable than your painful automatic thoughts, and how to start making action plans based on your new, balanced thoughts.

In order to change patterns of limited thinking, it's helpful to recognize and identify them, so we'll start by explaining some of the most common types. The remainder of the chapter is devoted to explaining how to use your Thought Journal to identify the patterns you tend to use and develop more balanced thoughts to counter them.

Identify the Eight Patterns

Here are eight of the most common patterns of limited thinking. It helps to study them separately, one at a time. However, in your ongoing stream of consciousness these patterns often occur in rapid succession, overlapping and blending into each other.

Filtering

Filtering is characterized by a sort of tunnel vision: looking at only one element of a situation to the exclusion of everything else. A single detail becomes the focus, and the whole event or situation is colored by this detail. For example, a computer draftsman who was uncomfortable with criticism was praised for his quality drawings and asked to get the next job out a little more quickly. He went home depressed, having decided that his employer thought he was dawdling. He filtered out the praise and focused only on the criticism.

Each person looks through their own particular tunnel. Depressed people are hypersensitive to loss and blind to gain. For anxious people, the slightest possibility of danger seems like a bomb threat even though the scene might otherwise be safe and secure. People who experience chronic anger look through a tunnel that highlights evidence of injustice and screens out fairness and equity.

Memory can also be very selective. You may remember only certain kinds of events from your entire life history. When you filter your memories, you often pass over positive experiences and dwell on memories that leave you angry, anxious, or depressed.

Filtering "awfulizes" your thoughts by pulling negative events out of context and focusing on them while ignoring your good experiences. Your fears, losses, and irritations become exaggerated in importance because they fill your awareness to the exclusion of everything else. Key words for the filtering pattern are "terrible," "awful," "disgusting," "scary," and so on. A key phrase is "I can't stand it."

Polarized Thinking

Polarized thinking is sometimes called black-and-white thinking. In this limited thinking pattern, no shades of gray are allowed. You insist on either-or choices, perceiving everything at the extremes with very little room for a middle ground. People and things are good or bad, wonderful or horrible, delightful or intolerable. Since your interpretations are extreme, your emotional reactions are extreme, fluctuating from despair to elation to rage to ecstasy to terror.

The greatest danger in polarized thinking is its impact on how you judge yourself. You could believe that if you aren't perfect or brilliant, then you must be a failure or an imbecile. There's no room for mistakes or mediocrity. For example, a charter bus driver told himself he was a real loser when he took the wrong freeway exit and had to drive two miles out of his way. One mistake meant that he was incompetent and worthless.

Similarly, a single mother with three children was determined to be strong and in charge. The moment she felt tired or nervous, she began thinking of herself as weak and falling apart, and she often criticized herself in conversations with friends.

Overgeneralization

In overgeneralization, you make broad conclusions based on a single incident or piece of evidence. One dropped stitch leads you to conclude, "I'll never learn how to knit." You interpret a rejection on the dance floor as "Nobody would ever want to dance with me."

This pattern can lead to an increasingly restricted life. If you got sick on a train once, you decide never to take a train again. If you got dizzy on a sixth-floor balcony, you never go out on balconies again. If you felt anxious the last time your husband took a business trip, you'll be a wreck every time he leaves town. One bad experience means that whenever you're in a similar situation, you will repeat the bad experience.

Overgeneralizations are often couched in the form of absolute statements, as if there were some immutable law that governs and limits your chances for happiness. Some of the cue words that indicate you may be overgeneralizing are "all," "every," "none," "never," "always," "everybody," and "nobody." For example, you are overgeneralizing when you make sweeping conclusions such as the following: "Nobody loves me," "I'll never be able to trust anyone again," "I will always be sad," "I've always had lousy jobs," "No one would stay friends with me if they really knew me."

Another hallmark of overgeneralization is applying global labels to people, places, and things you don't like. Somebody who refused to give you a ride home is labeled a "total jerk." A quiet guy on a date is a "dull clam." Democrats are "knee-jerk liberals." New York City is "hell on earth." Television is an "evil, corrupting influence." You're "stupid" and "totally wasting your life." Each of these labels may contain a grain of truth, but it generalizes that grain into a global judgment that ignores all contrary evidence, making your view of the world stereotyped and one-dimensional.

Mind Reading

When you mind read, you assume you know how others are feeling and what motivates them, which can lead to snap judgments: "He's just acting that way because he's jealous," "She's only interested in your money," "He's afraid to show he cares."

If your brother, who recently broke up with his girlfriend, visits a new woman acquaintance three times in one week, there are any number of conclusions you might arrive at; for example, that he's in love, angry at his old girlfriend and hoping she'll find out, on the rebound, or afraid of being alone again. Without asking, you have no way of knowing which is true. Mind reading makes one conclusion seem so obviously correct that you assume it's true, act on it inappropriately, and get into trouble.

With mind reading, you also make assumptions about how people are reacting to you. You might assume what your boyfriend is thinking and say to yourself, "This close, he sees how unattractive I am." If he's mind reading too, he may be saying to himself, "She thinks I'm really immature." You may have a casual encounter with your supervisor at work and come away thinking, "She's getting ready to fire me." These assumptions are born of intuition, hunches, vague misgivings, or a couple of past experiences. They are untested and unproven, but you believe them nonetheless.

Mind reading arises from a process called projection. You imagine that people feel the same way you do and react to things the same way you do. Therefore, you don't watch or listen closely enough to notice that others are actually different. If you get angry when someone is late, you imagine everyone feels that way. If you feel excruciatingly sensitive to rejection, you expect that most people are the same. If you are very judgmental about particular habits and traits, you assume others share your beliefs.

Catastrophizing

If you catastrophize, a small leak in the sailboat means it will surely sink. A contractor whose estimate gets underbid concludes he'll never get another job. A headache suggests that brain cancer is looming.

Catastrophic thoughts often start with the words "what if." You read a newspaper article describing a tragedy or hear gossip about some disaster befalling an acquaintance, and you start wondering, "What if it happens to me?" "What if I break my leg skiing?" "What if they hijack my plane?" "What if I get sick and have to go on disability?" "What if my son starts taking drugs?" The list is endless. There are no limits to an active catastrophic imagination.

Magnifying

When you magnify, you emphasize things out of proportion to their actual importance. Small mistakes become tragic failures. Minor suggestions become scathing criticism. A slight backache becomes a ruptured disk. Minor setbacks are cause for despair. Slight obstacles seem like overwhelming barriers. Words like "huge," "impossible," and "overwhelming" are magnifying terms. This pattern creates a tone of doom and hysterical pessimism.

The flip side of magnifying is minimizing. When you magnify, you view everything negative and difficult in your life through a telescope that enlarges your problems. But when you view your assets, such as your ability to cope and find solutions, you look through the wrong end of the telescope, so everything positive is minimized.

Personalization

There are two kinds of personalization. One involves directly comparing yourself with other people: "He plays piano so much better than I do," "I'm not smart enough to go with this crowd," "She knows herself a lot better than I do," "He feels things so deeply, while I'm dead inside," "I'm the slowest person in the office."

Sometimes the comparison is actually favorable to you: "He's dumb (and I'm smart)," "I'm better looking than she is." The opportunities for comparison never end. And even when the comparison is favorable, the underlying assumption is that your worth is questionable.

Consequently, you must continue to test your value, constantly measuring yourself against others. If you come out better, you have a moment's relief. If you come up short, you feel diminished.

This chapter began with an example of the other kind of personalization: the tendency to relate everything around you to yourself. A depressed parent blames themself when they see any sadness in their children. A businessperson thinks that every time a partner complains of being tired, it means she's tired of being in business with him. A man whose spouse complains of rising prices hears the complaints as attacks on his ability to provide for the family.

Shoulds

You may operate from a list of inflexible rules about how you and other people should act, and view these rules as right and indisputable. You see any deviation from your values or standards as bad, and as a result, you often judge others and find fault. People irritate you. They don't act correctly, and they don't think correctly. They have unacceptable traits, habits, and opinions that make them hard to tolerate. They should know the rules, and they should follow them.

One woman felt that her husband should want to take her on Sunday drives. She decided that a man who loves his wife ought to take her to the country and then out to eat at a nice place. The fact that he didn't want to meant he only thought about himself. Cue words indicating the presence of this pattern are "should," "ought," and "must." In fact, therapist Albert Ellis dubbed this thinking pattern "musterbation."

Your shoulds are just as hard on you as they are on other people. You feel compelled to be or act a certain way, but you never ask objectively if it really makes sense. Psychiatrist Karen Horney called this the "tyranny of shoulds." Here is a list of some of the most common and unreasonable shoulds. *I should:*

- be the epitome of generosity, consideration, dignity, courage, and unselfishness.

- be the perfect lover, friend, parent, teacher, student, or spouse.

- be able to endure any hardship with equanimity.

- be able to find a quick solution to every problem.

- never feel hurt. I should always be happy and serene.

- know, understand, and foresee everything.

- always be spontaneous but also always control my feelings.

- never feel certain emotions, such as anger or jealousy.

- love all of my children equally.

- never make mistakes.

- always feel love once I fall in love, as my emotions should be constant.

- be totally self-reliant.

- assert myself but never hurt anybody else.

- never be tired or get sick.

- always be at peak efficiency.

Balanced Alternatives

There are alternative responses to the eight patterns of limited thinking. You can use this list as a reference when you're having problems with a particular pattern.

Filtering

You have been stuck in a mental groove, focusing on things from your environment that typically frighten, sadden, or anger you. In order to conquer filtering, you will have to deliberately shift focus. You can shift focus in two ways.

One approach is to place your attention on coping strategies for dealing with the problem rather than obsessing about the problem itself.

The other is to focus on the opposite of your primary mental theme. For example, if you tend to focus on the theme of loss, instead focus on what you still have that is of value. If your theme is danger, focus instead on things in your environment that represent comfort and safety. If your theme is injustice, stupidity, or incompetence, shift your focus to what people do that does meet with your approval.

Polarized Thinking

The key to overcoming polarized thinking is to stop making black-or-white judgments. People are not either happy or sad, loving or rejecting, brave or cowardly, smart or stupid. They fall somewhere along a continuum between these extremes. Human beings are just too complex to be reduced to either-or judgments.

If you have to make these kinds of ratings, think in terms of percentages: "About 30 percent of me is scared to death, and 70 percent is holding on and coping," "About 60 percent of the time he seems terribly preoccupied with himself, but 40 percent of the time he can be really generous," "About 5 percent of the time I'm an ignoramus, but the rest of the time I do all right."

Overgeneralization

Overgeneralization is exaggeration—the tendency to take a button and sew a vest on it. Fight it by quantifying instead of using words like "huge," "awful," "massive," "minuscule," and so on. For example, if you catch yourself thinking, "We're buried under massive debt," rephrase with a quantity: "We owe $47,000."

Another way to avoid overgeneralization is to examine how much evidence you really have for your conclusion. If the conclusion is based on one or two cases, a single mistake, or one small symptom, throw it out until you have more convincing proof. This is such a powerful technique that most of the next chapter is devoted to amassing evidence for and against your hot thoughts.

Stop thinking in absolutes by avoiding words such as "every," "all," "always," "none," "never," "everybody," and "nobody." Statements that include these words ignore the exceptions and shades of gray. Replace absolutes with words such as "may," "sometimes," and "often."

Be particularly sensitive to absolute predictions about the future, such as "No one will ever love me." They are extremely dangerous because, as you behave in accordance with them, they can become self-fulfilling prophecies.

Pay close attention to the words you use to describe yourself and others. Replace frequently used negative labels with more neutral terms. For example, if you call your habitual caution "cowardice," replace it with "care." Think of your excitable mother as vivacious instead of ditzy. Instead of blaming yourself for being lazy, call yourself laid-back.

Mind Reading

In the long run, you are probably better off making no inferences about people at all. Either believe what they tell you or hold no belief about their thoughts and motivations until conclusive evidence comes your way. Treat all your notions about people as hypotheses to be tested and checked out by asking them.

Sometimes you can't check out your interpretations. For instance, you may not be ready to ask your daughter if her withdrawal from family life means she's pregnant or taking drugs. But you can allay your anxiety by generating alternative interpretations of her behavior. Perhaps she's in love, studying hard, depressed about something, deeply engrossed in a project, or worrying about her future.

By generating a string of possibilities, you may find a more neutral interpretation that's as likely to be true as your direst suspicions. This process also underlines the fact that you really can't know accurately what others are thinking and feeling unless they tell you.

Catastrophizing

Catastrophizing is the royal road to anxiety. As soon as you catch yourself catastrophizing, ask yourself, "What are the odds?" Make an honest assessment of the situation in terms of odds or percent of probability. Are the chances of disaster 1 in 100,000 (0.001 percent), 1 in 1,000 (0.1 percent), or 1 in 20 (5 percent)? Looking at the odds helps you realistically evaluate whatever is frightening you.

Magnifying

To combat magnifying, stop using words like "terrible," "awful," "disgusting," "horrendous," and so on. In particular, banish phrases like "I can't stand it," "It's impossible," and "It's unbearable."

You can stand it, because history shows that human beings can survive almost any psychological blow and can endure incredible physical pain. You can get used to and cope with almost anything. Try saying phrases such as "I can cope" and "I can survive this" to yourself instead.

Personalization

If you assume that the reactions of others are often about you, force yourself to check it out. Maybe the reason your boss is frowning isn't that you're late. Make no conclusion unless you are satisfied that you have reasonable evidence and proof.

When you catch yourself comparing yourself to others, remind yourself that everyone has strong and weak points. By matching your weak points to the corresponding strong points of others, you're just looking for ways to demoralize yourself.

The fact is, human beings are too complex for casual comparisons to have any meaning. It would take you months to catalog and compare all the thousands of traits and abilities of two people.

Shoulds

Reexamine and question any personal rules or expectations that include the words "should," "ought," or "must." Flexible rules and expectations don't use these words because there are always exceptions and special circumstances. Think of at least three exceptions to your rule, and then imagine all the exceptions there must be that you can't think of.

You may get irritated when people don't act according to your values. But your personal values are just that—personal. They may work for you, but as missionaries have discovered all over the world, they don't always work for others. People aren't all the same.

The key is to focus on each person's uniqueness—his or her particular needs, limitations, fears, and pleasures. Because it is impossible to know all of these complex interrelations, even with intimates, you can't be certain whether your values apply to another. You are entitled to an opinion, but allow for the possibility that you may be wrong. Also, allow other people to find different things important.

Combat Patterns

Now that you've learned to identify limited thinking patterns, and are aware of alternatives, it's time to apply your new skill to the Thought Journal you started. You can use the downloadable and printable worksheet from http://www.newharbinger.com/ 48695, or simply draw a three-column chart in your journal.

Start by analyzing your most distressing automatic thoughts to see which limited thinking pattern is most characteristic of each. Write them in the first column. You may find evidence of more than one limited thinking pattern. Write down all that apply.

In the next column, rewrite your automatic thoughts in a more balanced way, or compose an alternative thought that refutes the automatic thought.

In the last column, rate your feeling again after you've worked on countering your automatic thoughts, using the same scale of 0 to 100, in which 0 means the feeling causes no distress and 100 is the most distressing emotion you have ever felt. The feeling should be less intense as a result of your work.

Action Plans

Your balanced or alternative thoughts may suggest actions you can take, such as:

- checking out assumptions
- gathering information
- making an assertive request
- clearing up misunderstandings
- making plans
- changing your schedule
- resolving unfinished business
- making commitments

Circle any action items in your second column and plan when you'll put them into action.

It may feel difficult, time-consuming, or embarrassing to follow your action plan. You may have to break your plan down into a series of easier steps and schedule each step. But it's worth doing.

Behavior that is inspired by your balanced or alternative thoughts will greatly reduce the frequency and power of your negative automatic thoughts.

—

Using your Thought Journal to identify balanced alternatives and create action plans is essential. It's the basic skill you need to master in order to use cognitive therapy to reduce painful feelings like anxiety and depression.

Most people make progress during the first week of faithfully keeping a Thought Journal. The longer you practice tuning in to your automatic thoughts, the better you get at it. It's a skill like knitting, skiing, writing, or singing on key: Practice makes perfect.

Chapter 3

HOT
THOUGHTS

If the techniques in the previous chapter worked well for you, it may not be necessary for you to work through this chapter. If, however, you had difficulty identifying your patterns of limited thinking, this chapter offers an alternative approach based on evidence gathering and analysis—a powerful weapon against automatic thoughts.

Hot thoughts are the thoughts that trigger emotion. This chapter will give you skills to do three things: identify the evidence that supports your hot (or trigger) thoughts; uncover evidence that contradicts your hot thoughts; and synthesize this information to create a healthier, more realistic perspective.

To master this skill, use a Thought and Evidence Journal that will allow you to record and analyze the evidence for and against your hot thoughts. You can download this from http://www.newharbinger.com/48695, or write out the prompts in your own journal. As before, make copies of the blank form and carry one with you at all times for at least the next week. Here's a brief outline of the process, followed by detailed instructions for how to use the form.

1. Select a hot thought.

2. Identify evidence that supports your hot thought.

3. Uncover evidence against your hot thought.

4. Write your balanced or alternative thoughts.

5. Rate your mood again.

6. Record and save alternative thoughts.

7. Practice your balanced thoughts.

8. Develop an action plan.

1: Select a Hot Thought

Return to your Thought Journal to select a hot thought from your record of automatic thoughts. Choose several thoughts that had a major impact on your mood because of either their power or their frequency. Rate how strongly each thought contributed to your painful feelings using a scale of 0 to 100, in which

100 indicates that the thought was solely responsible for your feelings. Circle the thought with the highest score; that's the one you'll work on now.

To help illustrate this approach, we'll take some examples from Len, a rep for a large printing company whose customers are mostly publishers and advertising companies. When Len rated all of his automatic thoughts using the scale of 0 to 100, "I'm a first-class failure" turned out to be his hottest thought by far. By itself, the thought could hit Len hard enough to stir up strong feelings of inadequacy and depression.

2: Identify Evidence For

Once you've identified your hot thought, record it on your downloaded Thought and Evidence Journal, including your ratings of the feeling and associated thoughts. Then, write down the experiences and facts that seem to support your hot thought.

This is not the place to put your feelings, impressions, assumptions about the reactions of others, or unsupported beliefs. In the "Evidence for" column, stay with the objective facts. Confine yourself to exactly what was said, what was done, how many times, and so on.

While it's important to stick with the facts, it's also important to acknowledge all of the past and present evidence that supports and verifies your hot thought.

Len identified five pieces of evidence that seemed to support the hot thought "I'm a first-class failure." Here's what he wrote in his "Evidence for" column:

- *Only $24,000 in sales for December.*

- *Couldn't close that big account when they seemed almost ready to give me the contract.*

- *Boss asked if I had any problems.*

- *This is the third time in twelve months I've been below $30,000 in sales.*

- *Had a disagreement with Randolph, and he pulled his job.*

Notice that Len doesn't talk about conjectures, assumptions, or a "feeling" that he's doing a bad job. He confines himself to the facts and an objective description of events.

3: Uncover Evidence Against

Coming up with evidence against your hot thought will probably be the hardest part of the technique. It's easy to think of things that support your hot thought, but you're likely to draw a blank when it's time to explore evidence against it, and you may need some help.

To assist you in the search for evidence against your hot thought, there are ten key questions you need to ask. Go through all ten questions for every hot thought you're analyzing. Each will help you explore new ways of thinking:

1. Is there an *alternative interpretation* of the situation, other than your hot thought?

2. Is the hot thought really *accurate*, or is it an overgeneralization? In Len's case, do low sales figures in December necessarily mean he's a failure?

3. Are there *exceptions* to the generalizations made by your hot thought?

4. Are there *balancing realities* that might soften negative aspects of the situation? In Len's case, are there other things besides sales that he can feel good about in his job?

5. What are the more *probable consequences* and outcomes of the situation? This question helps you differentiate what you fear might happen from what you can reasonably expect will happen.

6. Are there *experiences from your past* that would lead you to a conclusion other than your hot thought?

7. Are there *objective facts* that would contradict items in the "Evidence for" column? Is it really true, for example, that Len lost that big contract because he was a failure as a salesman?

8. What are the *real odds* that what you fear will actually occur? Think like a bookie: are the odds 1 in 2, 1 in 50, 1 in 1,000, 1 in 500,000? Consider all the people right now in this same situation; how many of them will end up facing the catastrophic outcome you fear?

9. Do you have the social or problem-solving *skills* to handle the situation differently?

10. Could you *create a plan* to change the situation? Perhaps there is someone you know who might deal with this differently. What would that person do?

On a separate piece of paper, write your answers to all of the questions relevant to your hot thought. It may take some thinking to:

- find exceptions to the generalization created by your hot thought

- objectively evaluate the odds of something catastrophic happening

- recall balancing realities that can give you confidence and hope in the face of problems.

Don't be tempted to take shortcuts or rush through this step in the evidence-gathering process. The work you put in is key in developing the ability to challenge hot thoughts. Here's what Len's process looked like.

Len spent more than half an hour answering the ten questions. They helped him come up with these statements for the "Evidence against" column:

- *December's normally a low month. That might explain most of my drop-off in sales.* (Question 1)

- *To be accurate, for the year overall I ranked fourth of the nine reps. That's not great, but it's not being a failure.* (Question 2)

- *Some months have been good. I did $68,000 in August and $64,000 in March.* (Question 3)

- *I have good relationships with many customers. In some cases I've really helped them with major decisions. Most know they can trust me as an advisor.* (Question 4)

- *My sales are good enough at number four in the company that they wouldn't fire me. (Question 5)*

- *Five years ago I was ranked number two, and I'm always in the top half of the pack. Over the years, there have been a lot of months when I got the best salesman award. (Question 6)*

- *I was just outbid on that big account. It wasn't my fault. (Question 7)*

- *Randolph said he wanted recycled paper and pulled the job when he didn't like the price. That's not my fault. (Question 7)*

- *I need to think more about my relationship with each customer and less about the dollar worth of each contract. From experience, I know that works better for me. (Question 10)*

Len found it particularly useful to look for objective facts that either counterbalanced or contradicted each item in the "Evidence for" column. He kept asking himself, "What in my experience balances out this piece of evidence?" and "What objective facts contradict this piece of evidence?"

Len was surprised at how much he discovered to write in the "Evidence against" column. This helped him realize that he tended to shut a lot of things out of his awareness when he was feeling depressed.

4: Write Balanced Alternatives

Now it's time to synthesize everything you've learned in both the "Evidence for" and "Evidence against" columns. Read over both columns slowly and carefully. Don't try to deny or ignore evidence on either side. Then write new, balanced thoughts that incorporate what you learned as you gathered the evidence. In your balanced thoughts it's okay to acknowledge important items in the "Evidence for" column, but it's equally important to summarize the main things you learned in the "Evidence against" column.

Here's what Len wrote in the "Balanced or alternative thoughts" column in his Thought and Evidence Journal:

My sales are down and I've lost two deals, but I have a solid sales record over the years and have had a lot of good months. I just need to focus on my customer relationships and not the money.

Notice that Len didn't ignore or deny that sales were down, but he was able to use items from his "Evidence against" column to develop a clear, balanced statement that acknowledged his track record as a competent salesman.

Synthesizing statements don't have to be long, but they do need to summarize the main points on both sides of the question. Don't hesitate to rewrite your new, balanced thought several times until the statement feels strong and convincing.

When you're satisfied with the accuracy of what you've written, rate your belief in this new balanced thought as a percentage ranging from 0 to 100. Len rated his belief in his new balanced thought at 85 percent.

If you don't believe your new thought more than 60 percent, you should revise it further, perhaps incorporating more items from the "Evidence against" column.

It's also possible that the evidence you've gathered isn't yet convincing enough, so you need to develop more ideas for the "Evidence against" column.

5: Rate Your Mood Again

It's time to find out where all of this work has gotten you. As part of your Thought Journal, you identified a painful feeling and rated its intensity on a scale of 0 to 100. Now rate the intensity of that same feeling again to see if it has changed as a result of the evidence you gathered and the new, balanced thought you developed.

Len found that his depression was much less intense after he went through this process, declining from 85 to 30 on the scale of 0 to 100. Most of the remaining depression seemed to be based on a realistic concern about reduced income due to his low December sales.

Seeing your mood change can be a strong reinforcement for continuing to work with the Thought and Evidence Journal, as you confront powerful hot thoughts and make positive changes in how you feel.

6: Record and Save Alternatives

We encourage you to record what you learn each time you examine the evidence and develop balanced or alternative thoughts. It's helpful to put this information on index cards that you can keep with you and read whenever you wish.

On one side of the card, write a description of the problem situation and your hot thought. On the other side, write your alternative or balanced thought. Over time, you may create a number of these cards. They can be a valuable resource for reminding you of your new, healthier thoughts when upsetting circumstances might cause you to forget them.

7: Practice Balanced Thoughts

You can use your index cards in a simple exercise that will give you practice with your balanced thoughts. Start by reading the side of the card that describes the triggering situation and your hot thought.

Then work at forming a clear visualization of the situation: Picture the scene, see the shapes and colors, and be aware of who is there and what they look like. Hear the voices and other sounds that are part of the scene. Notice the temperature. Notice if you're touching anything and what it feels like. Using all five senses makes your scene much more vivid.

When the image of the scene is very clear, read your hot thought. Try to focus on it to the point of having an emotional reaction. When you can picture the scene clearly and feel some of the emotions that go with it, turn the card over and read your balanced thoughts. Think of the balanced thoughts while continuing to visualize the scene, and continue to pair the balanced thoughts with the scene until your emotional reaction subsides.

Len did this exercise by picturing the monthly sales notice while thinking his hot thought "I'm a first-class failure." After feeling a small surge of depression, he paired the image of the sales report with the balanced thoughts described earlier. It took several minutes of focusing on the balanced thoughts before his depression started to subside.

One of the important things Len learned from this exercise was that he could both increase and decrease his depression by focusing on key thoughts. You can too.

8: Develop an Action Plan

As with the Thought Journal, you can use the Thought and Evidence Journal to help you develop action plans.

Study the "Evidence against" column and look for an item that involves using coping skills or implementing a plan to handle the situation differently. Circle any items that suggest a plan of action. Write three specific steps you could take to implement your action plan in the problem situation.

Len's action plan focused on his decision to think about customer relationships rather than the dollar value of each contract. Here's what he decided to do:

Send New Year's greetings to all of my regular customers.

Call each customer with a request for feedback about how I and my company could improve service.

Focus on enjoying my customers as people; for example, taking the time to chat instead of pushing quickly to business.

Additional Tips

The Thought and Evidence Journal is a powerful tool against automatic thoughts, but you need to proceed systematically through all the steps. Here are a few tips to help you overcome some common obstacles to success:

- If you have more than one strong hot thought, do a separate Thought and Evidence Journal for each.

- If you have difficulty developing alternative interpretations to the hot thought (Question 1), imagine how a friend or an objective observer might look at the situation.

- If you have difficulty identifying exceptions to generalizations made by your hot thought (Question 3), think of times you've been in the situation without anything negative happening. Perhaps you even experienced something positive: Was there a time when you handled the situation particularly well? Were you ever praised in the situation?

- If you have difficulty remembering objective facts to counteract items in the "Evidence for" column (Question 7), you might ask a friend or family member to help you.

- If you have difficulty assessing the odds of a feared outcome (Question 8), make an estimate of all the times in the last year someone in the United States has been in this same situation and how many times the feared catastrophe has occurred.

- If you have difficulty making an action plan (Question 10), imagine how a very competent friend or acquaintance would handle the same situation. What would he or she do, say, or try that might create a different outcome?

—

Using the Thought and Evidence Journal described in this chapter, you can make significant changes in your moods in as little as one week. However, it will take from two to twelve weeks to consolidate your gains, as your new, more balanced thoughts gain strength through repetition.

Chapter 4

RELAXATION

Relaxation training differs from what we normally think of as relaxing. It's more than watching a movie to take your mind off things or going for a long, quiet walk to unwind. When psychologists talk about learning to relax, they are referring to regularly practicing one or more of a group of specific relaxation exercises. These exercises often involve a combination of deep breathing, muscle relaxation, and visualization techniques that have been proven to release the muscular tension that the body stores during times of stress.

During your relaxation training sessions, you will discover that racing thoughts start to slow and feelings of fear and anxiety ease considerably. In fact, when your body is completely relaxed, it's impossible to feel fear or anxiety.

In what is called the relaxation response, heart rate, breath rate, blood pressure, skeletal muscle tension, metabolic rate, oxygen consumption, and skin electrical conductivity all decrease. On the other hand, alpha brain-wave frequency, which is associated with a state of calm well-being, increases. Every one of these physical conditions is exactly opposite to reactions that anxiety and fear produce in the body. Deep relaxation and anxiety are physiological opposites

This chapter focuses on highly effective techniques that, when practiced regularly, can bring about deep states of relaxation.

Initially, you'll want to do your relaxation training in a quiet room where you won't be disturbed. Wear loose, nonbinding clothing. At the start of each exercise, assume a comfortable position, either lying down or sitting, in which your body feels well supported. If you wish, you can use white noise, such as a white noise machine or the humming of a fan, to cover up sounds that you have no control over.

Later, when you're more familiar with the exercises, you can try them in more distracting settings and public places.

Abdominal Breathing

One group of muscles that commonly tenses in response to stress are those located in the wall of your abdomen. When your abdominal muscles are tight, they push against your diaphragm as it extends downward to initiate each breath. This pushing action restricts the amount of air you take in and forces the air you do inhale to remain in the top part of your lungs.

If your breathing is high and shallow, you'll probably feel as though you aren't getting enough oxygen. This is stressful and sets off mental alarms that you are in danger. To make up for the lack of air, instead of relaxing your abdominal muscles and taking deeper breaths, you may take quick, shallow breaths. This shallow, rapid breathing can lead you to hyperventilate—one of the prime causes of panic.

Abdominal breathing reverses this process by relaxing the muscles that press against your diaphragm and slowing your breath rate. Three or four deep abdominal breaths can be an almost instant relaxer.

Abdominal breathing is usually easy to learn. Practice the following exercise for about ten minutes to acquire this simple but extremely effective skill:

1. Lie down and close your eyes. Take a moment to notice the sensations in your body, particularly where your body is holding any tension. Take several breaths

and see what you notice about the quality of your breathing. Where is your breath centered? Are your lungs expanding fully? Does your chest move in and out when you breathe? Does your abdomen? Do both?

2. Place one hand on your chest and the other on your abdomen, right below your waist. As you breathe in, imagine that you're sending your breath as far down into your body as it will go. Feel your lungs expand as they fill up with air. As you do this, the hand on your chest should remain fairly still, and the hand on your abdomen should rise and fall with each breath. If you have difficulty getting the hand on your abdomen to move, or if both hands are moving, try gently pressing down with the hand on your abdomen. As you breathe, direct the air so it pushes up against the pressure of your hand, forcing it to rise.

3. Continue to gently breathe in and out. Let your breath find its own pace. If your

breathing feels unnatural or forced in any way, just maintain your awareness of that sensation as you breathe in and out. Eventually any straining or unnaturalness should ease up by itself.

4. After breathing deeply for several breaths, begin to count each time you exhale. After ten exhalations, start the count over with one. When thoughts intrude and you lose track of the number you are on, simply return your attention to the exercise and start counting again from one. Continue counting your breaths for ten minutes, with some awareness devoted to ensuring that the hand on your abdomen continues to rise with each breath.

Progressive Muscle Relaxation

Progressive muscle relaxation (PMR) is a relaxation technique that involves tensing and relaxing all the various muscle groups in your body in a specific sequence. The body responds to anxious and fearful thoughts by storing tension in the muscles. This tension can be released by consciously tightening the muscles beyond their normal tension point and then suddenly relaxing them. Repeating this procedure with every muscle group in the body can induce a deep state of relaxation.

If you practice PMR as offered in this book, you'll experience the physical benefits of the relaxation response. More importantly, if you continue to regularly practice PMR for several months, the amount of anxiety, anger, or other painful emotions that habitually come up in your life will significantly diminish.

A simple regimen of exercises can be effective. These exercises divide the body into four major muscle groups: the arms, head, midsection, and legs.

Practice the following exercise for about twenty or thirty minutes daily, whether you feel like it or not. You are developing a skill: the ability to relax. In the beginning, you may find that it takes you a long time to relax even a little bit. However, as you continue to practice, you'll learn to relax more deeply and more rapidly.

Shorthand Muscle Relaxation

Although the basic PMR procedure is an excellent way to relax, it takes so long to go through all the different muscle groups sequentially that it isn't a practical tool for on-the-spot relaxation. To relax your body quickly, you need to learn the following shorthand PMR method.

The key to shorthand PMR is learning to simultaneously relax the muscles in each of the four body areas. You will tense and hold each group for seven seconds, then allow that entire group of muscles to relax for twenty seconds. As you become more adept, you may need less time for both tensing and relaxing. Here are the steps for shorthand PMR:

1. Make tight fists while flexing your biceps and forearms. Hold the tension for seven seconds, then relax for twenty seconds.

2. Press your head back as far as you can. Roll it clockwise once, in a complete circle, then roll it counterclockwise once. As you do this, wrinkle up your face as though you were trying to make every part of it meet at

your nose. Relax. Next, tense your jaw and throat muscles and hunch your shoulders up, then relax.

3. Gently arch your back as you take a deep breath. Hold this position, then relax. Take another deep breath, and this time push your abdomen out as you inhale, then relax.

4. Point your toes up toward your face while tightening your calf and shin muscles, then relax. Next, curl your toes while tightening your calf, thigh, and buttock muscles, then relax.

Relaxation without Tension

Within seven to fourteen PMR practice sessions, you should be adept at recognizing and releasing tension in your muscles. After that, you may not need to deliberately contract each muscle group before you relax it.

Instead, scan your body for tension by running your attention through the four areas of the body in sequence.

If you find any tightness, simply let go of it, just as you did after each contraction in the PMR exercises. Stay focused and really feel each sensation. Work with each muscle group until the muscles seem completely relaxed. If you come to an area that feels tight and won't let go, tighten that one muscle or muscle group and then release the tension.

This method is even faster than the PMR shorthand procedure. It's also a good way to relax sore muscles that you don't want to aggravate by overtensing.

Cue-Controlled Relaxation

In cue-controlled relaxation, you learn to relax your muscles whenever you want by combining a verbal suggestion with abdominal breathing.

First, get in a comfortable position, and then release as much tension as you can using the technique for relaxing without tension we just described. Focus on your belly as it moves in and out with each breath, and make your breaths slow and rhythmic. With each breath, let yourself become more and more relaxed.

Then, on every inhalation, say the words "breathe in" to yourself, and as you exhale, say the word "relax." Just keep saying to yourself, "breathe in...relax...breathe in...relax," while letting go of tension throughout your body. Continue this practice for five minutes, repeating the cue words with each breath.

The cue-controlled method teaches your body to associate the word "relax" with the feeling of relaxation. After you have practiced this technique for a while and the association is strong, you'll be able to relax your muscles anytime, anywhere, just by mentally repeating, "breathe in...relax," and releasing any feelings of tightness throughout your body.

Cue-controlled relaxation can give you stress relief in less than a minute and is a major component of the treatment plans for anxiety and anger management.

Visualizing a Peaceful Scene

Another way to relax is by mentally constructing a peaceful scene that you can enter whenever you feel stressed. Your peaceful scene should be a setting that you find interesting and appealing. It will be a place that

will make you feel safe and secure when you imagine it—
where you will be able to let your guard down and completely relax.

Finding Your Scene

Take a comfortable position, either sitting or lying
down, and for a few minutes practice cue-controlled
relaxation. Visualization is most effective when you are
completely relaxed, so be sure to take enough time to
relax thoroughly.

Now simply ask your unconscious to show you your
peaceful scene. A picture may start to form in your
imagination. Or, instead of an image, you may mentally
hear a word, phrase, or sound that will start to stir an
image to life. However it happens, if an image starts to
show itself, don't question it. Accept this as a setting
that has a restful resonance for you.

If a scene doesn't start to appear to you, choose a
place or an activity that appeals to you. Where would
you like to be right now? In the country, the woods, or a
meadow? On a boat? In a cabin? At the house where
you grew up? In a penthouse overlooking Central Park?

Once your imagination has settled on a scene, notice what objects you have around you in the scene. See their colors and shapes. What sounds do you hear? What scents are in the air? What are you doing? What physical sensations are you feeling? Try to notice everything about the scene.

You may find that parts of your scene remain unclear or hazy, no matter how hard you try to bring them into focus. This is perfectly normal. Don't be disappointed. With practice, you'll be able to draw out the details and make your scene more vivid.

Visualization Skills

Visualization is a skill. Like many skills, such as drawing, cabinet making, or sewing, some people are initially more adept at it than others. You may be a person who can sit down and re-create a scene so clearly that you feel like you're actually there. Or you might find it difficult to see anything at all.

Even if you aren't a natural at visualization, you can develop this skill with practice. The following guidelines will help you bring your visualizations to life.

Once an image appears, if there are any gaps in the scene—if one part seems hazy or void of any image at all—put all your concentration on that area and ask, "What is it?" Hold your attention on that area and see if it starts to clear. Even if the image is fuzzy or blank, watch whatever appears in your imagination as intently as you can.

It's important to make your imagined scene as real as possible. One way to accomplish this is by adding as much detail as you can gather from at least three of your five senses. Visually, you can bring out the shapes in your scene by running your attention over the outlines of the images as though you were tracing them with a pencil. Notice the colors in your scene. Are they vivid or faded? Locate the light source. How does the light falling on an object affect its color? What areas are in shadow? Try to notice everything you could actually see if you were there.

Pay attention to the information you would gather through your other senses. What sounds would you hear if you were actually there? What would the environment smell like? What can you feel through your sense of touch? Are there areas that are hot or cold? Is a breeze blowing? Imagine running your hand over various objects and notice their texture and the sensations this action creates in your body.

Observe the perspective from which you're viewing the scene. Are you viewing it as though you're an outsider looking in? The clue to the "outside looking in" perspective is when you actually see an imagined "you" in your scene. If you do, you need to shift perspective so that your view is what you'd see if you were actually in the scene. For example, if your peaceful scene involves lying underneath some trees, instead of seeing yourself reclining on the ground, shift your perspective so you see the branches of the trees against a clear blue sky. By seeing things from a perspective inside the scene, you'll draw yourself completely into the image and are more likely to feel that you're living the scene rather than just viewing it.

When unrelated thoughts intrude, notice their content and then return your attention to the scene you're creating.

Examples of Scenes

Here are a few examples that may give you an idea of how to put your peaceful scenes together. Adopt the details that appeal to you and add others of your own that you find particularly relaxing.

THE BEACH. You have just descended a long flight of wooden stairs and now find yourself standing on a stretch of the most pristine beach you have ever seen. It is wide and stretches as far as you can see in either direction. You sit down on the sand and find that it's white, smooth, warm, and heavy. You let the sand sift through your fingers, and it seems almost liquid. You lie on your stomach and find that the warm sand instantly conforms to the shape of your body. A breeze touches your face. The soft sand holds you. The surf rumbles as it rises into long white crests that gently break toward you and then dissolve into the sand a few yards away from you. The air smells of salt and sea life, and you breathe it in deeply. You feel calm and safe.

THE FOREST. You are in a forest, lying down in a circle of very tall trees. Underneath you is a cushion of soft, dry moss. The air is strongly scented with laurel and pine, and the atmosphere feels deep, still, and serene. You drink in the warmth of the sun as it streams through the branches, dappling the carpet of moss. A warm breeze rises. The tall trees around you sway, and the leaves rustle rhythmically with each waft of wind. Each time the breeze swells, every muscle in your body becomes more relaxed. Two songbirds warble in the distance. A chipmunk chatters above. A sense of ease, peace, and joy spreads from head to toe.

THE TRAIN. You are riding in a private car at the very end of a long train. The entire ceiling of the car is a dome of tinted glass and the walls of the car are glass, creating the illusion that you are out in the open, flying through the vast countryside. A plush couch sits at the far end, with two overstuffed chairs opposite and a coffee table in the middle, complete with your favorite magazines. You sink deeply into one of the chairs, push off your shoes, and put your feet on the table. Outside there's an ever-receding panorama: mountains, trees, snowcapped peaks, a lake shimmering in the distance. The sun has almost set and the sky is awash in purples and reds, with towering red-orange clouds. As you gaze at these scenes, you ease into the rhythm of the clacking wheels and feel the lull of the rocking motion of the train.

———

Often, two or more methods can be combined to deepen your sense of relaxation; for instance, you could visualize a peaceful scene while practicing deep breathing. Abdominal breathing, progressive muscle relaxation, and relaxation without tension should be learned in sequence.

In general, you can experience the benefits of deep relaxation, using any of these methods, within a session or two.

Chapter 5

WORRY CONTROL

Everybody worries from time to time. It's a natural response to anticipated future problems. But when worry gets out of hand, it can become an almost full-time preoccupation. You have a serious problem with worry if you regularly experience any of the following:

- Chronic anxiety about future dangers or threats

- Consistently making negative predictions about the future

- Often overestimating the probability or seriousness of bad things happening

- Inability to stop repeating the same worries over and over

- Escaping worry by distracting yourself or avoiding certain situations

- Having difficulty using worry constructively to produce solutions to problems

People who tell you to just stop worrying don't realize how the human mind works. It's a famous psychological conundrum. Imagine we offered you a thousand dollars to not think of a white bear for a full minute. You might have gone for months or years without thinking about a white bear, but as soon as you decide to *not* think about it, you can't get that damned bear out of your mind. Just try it.

This chapter will teach you to control worry in four ways. First, it will direct you to *regularly practice* the relaxation techniques you learned in the last chapter. Second, it will teach you to conduct accurate *risk assessments* to counter any tendency to overestimate future danger. Third, it will teach you *worry exposure* to make worrying less distressing and more productive by doing all your worrying during a scheduled session.

Finally, this chapter also teaches *worry behavior prevention*, a technique for controlling ineffective strategies you may be using to reduce your worries somewhat in the short term that actually perpetuate them in the long term. For example, you'll discover ways to get places on time without obsessively checking your watch or circling the block because you're too early, or how to stop excessively calling to check up on loved ones about whom you worry too much.

Levels of Worry

Worry isn't just a mental process. When you worry, you enter into a cyclical pattern that involves your thoughts, body, and behavior, as shown in the diagram of the worry system below.

PANIC SEQUENCE EVENT
(External or Internal)

WORRY
(Anticipatory Thoughts: "I could have a panic attack.")

CATASTROPHIC THOUGHTS
ANXIETY-MAINTAINING THOUGHTS

PHYSIOLOGICAL SYMPTOMS
(Fight or Flight, Hyperventilation)

An event—for example, the sight of an ambulance or the thought of a loved one getting hurt—starts worry thoughts going, and you start feeling anxious.

On the *physical level,* your heart starts beating faster, your breathing quickens, your skin gets sweaty, your muscles tense, and you may have other physical symptoms associated with the fight-or-flight response.

On the *behavioral level,* you may take action to avoid the upsetting situation or place. Or you may begin checking behavior, such as calling to see if a loved one is all right or proofreading a report for the fifth time.

To control worry, you need to approach it on all these levels. First, you will deal with physical stress reactions by practicing relaxation exercises. To address the cognitive features of worry, you'll practice risk assessment and worry exposure. Then you'll get behavioral problems under control with worry behavior prevention.

Relaxation

You learned relaxation skills in the previous chapter. Chronic worry creates chronic muscular tension. By practicing relaxation daily, you can provide yourself with crucial breaks in the cycle of fight-or-flight reactions that worry causes.

Take the time once a day to perform the full progressive muscle-relaxation procedure. Set aside a dedicated time each day when, no matter what else is going on, you will do this exercise. It's important that you practice daily and not skip or shorten your sessions. Reaching a profound level of deep relaxation once a day is an important part of worry control that cannot be postponed. You can't catch up on it tomorrow if you skip it today.

Five times a day, at more or less regular intervals, do a quick cue-controlled relaxation. This only takes a moment, and you can do it anywhere. Frequent relaxing moments will keep your overall level of physical stress under control.

Risk Assessment

If worry is a problem for you, the skill and art of risk assessment can help. No one can escape risk in life. The trick is to know which risks you can avoid, which you should prepare for, and which you simply don't have to worry about. There are two main aspects of risk assessment: estimating probability and predicting outcomes.

Estimating Probability

People who worry a lot consistently overestimate risk. Some think there's a high chance of a traffic accident every time they start the car. Others worry excessively about making a mistake at work, even though they perform their job well and have seldom or never made a big mistake. Overestimation happens because of some combination of experience and belief: how much weight you give to your personal experience, and what beliefs you hold about the function of worry.

EXPERIENCE. There are two ways that your personal history can influence your worrying. One way is if nothing too bad has ever happened to you, but you ignore this historical evidence. It doesn't stop you from worrying about forgetting something important or losing a significant relationship. If you think this way, it seems every day that passes without disaster increases the odds of bad things happening.

The other way personal history influences worrying is if something bad did happen to you once and you give this historical evidence too much weight. You figure that anything that happened once is likely to happen again—that lightning not only strikes twice, but actually likes to strike the same spot over and over.

BELIEF. There are two ways that deeply held, unexamined beliefs can make worry worse. First, you might believe in the predictive power of worry. A man who worried about his husband leaving him believed that the fact that he thought about it a lot indicated that his partner was indeed likely to leave.

The second way belief can trap you is if you believe in the preventive power of worry. In this case, you unconsciously assume that bad things haven't happened to you because your worry about them has kept trouble at bay. You feel like a sentry on guard, ever vigilant.

The problem with these errors in estimating risk through experience and belief is that they subtly increase your worry until it becomes a bigger problem than the dangers you worry about. The way out of this trap is to learn accurate risk assessment.

Predicting Outcomes

Even if what you worry about comes to pass, will the outcome be as catastrophic as you fear? Most people who worry a lot consistently predict unreasonably catastrophic outcomes. This is catastrophizing. For example, a woman who worried about losing her job actually did lose her job. But instead of ending up homeless and poor, she got another job. It paid a little less, but she liked the work more. The catastrophic outcome she predicted didn't occur.

When you worry, your anxiety makes you forget that people routinely cope with even the most serious disasters. You forget that you and your family and friends will probably find a way to cope with whatever happens.

Rate Your Anxiety

You can create a Risk Assessment Worksheet in your journal or download one from our website at http://www.newharbinger.com/48695.

On the first line, record one of your worries in the form of a feared event. Write down the worst possible version of your worry you can think of. For example, if you worry about your teenager going out at night, imagine the worst: a head-on collision of drunk teens and a big truck, and everybody dead on impact or dying in the emergency room after suffering horribly.

Next, write the *automatic thoughts* that typically come up: "She'll die... I'll die... Blood and pain... Things will never be the same... Awful... Can't stand it..." Jot down whatever comes to mind, even if it's just an image or a fleeting word.

Now rate your anxiety when considering this worst-case scenario, using a scale of 0 to 100 where 0 is no anxiety and 100 is the worst fear you've ever experienced.

Then rate the probability of this worst-case scenario coming to pass, from 0 percent for no likelihood at all to 100 percent for absolute inevitability.

The next section deals with *catastrophic thinking*. Assuming that the worst did happen, predict the consequences you most fear. Then spend some time figuring out what you would tell yourself and what you would do in order to cope with the catastrophe. When you have a clear picture of possible coping strategies, make a revised prediction of the likely consequences if what you fear does come to pass. Then rate your anxiety again and see if it has diminished.

The next section addresses the issue of *overestimation*. List the evidence against the very worst outcome happening. Figure the odds as realistically as you can. Then list all of the alternative outcomes you can think of. Finally, once again rate your anxiety and the probability of the event. You should find that both your anxiety and your probability ratings have declined as the result of your doing this full and objective risk assessment.

Do this exercise whenever you're confronted by a significant worry or return to a worry more than once. It's important to do this exercise consistently. Each risk assessment helps you change old habits of catastrophic thinking. If you'd like to see an example, we've provided one filled out on our website at http://www.newharbinger.com/48695.

When you've completed a risk assessment, keep the exercise. You may wish to refer to it again when confronting a similar worry.

Worry Exposure

When practicing worry exposure, you expose yourself to minor worries first, experiencing them for thirty minutes at a time. When minor worries no longer cause you painful anxiety, you move on to more distressing worries. Gradually, you learn to take on your major worries with little or no anxiety.

Worry exposure is a form of prolonged imagery exposure, a technique that floods your imagination with fearful images until you grow tired of them. Given enough time and focused attention, even the most upsetting material becomes overly familiar and boring, making it less upsetting the next time you encounter it.

This effect doesn't happen when you simply worry on your own, because you don't spend enough time dwelling on only the worst possible outcome. When you do "free-form" worrying, without a structure, you try to distract yourself, argue with yourself, escape into another topic, perform ritual checking or avoiding behaviors, and so on, and therefore gain none of the benefits of structured worry exposure.

Schedule a thirty-minute period each day for full-scale, concentrated, organized worrying. You'll do all of your worrying then. If you're tempted to worry at any other time, you'll postpone it until your next scheduled worry exposure session. Worry exposure makes worrying less distressing and more productive.

Worry exposure also works well because it concentrates your worrying time. When you know that you'll be worrying intensely during your daily exposure session, it's easier to clear your mind of worry during the rest of the day.

Worry exposure consists of eight simple steps:

1. List your worries.

2. Rank your worries.

3. Relax.

4. Visualize a worry.

5. Rate your peak anxiety from 0 to 100.

6. Imagine alternative outcomes.

7. Rate your anxiety from 0 to 100 again.

8. Repeat steps 4 through 7.

1: List Your Worries

Write a list of the things you typically worry about. Include worries about success and failure, holding relationships together, performance at school or work, physical danger, health, making mistakes, rejection, shame over past events, and so on.

2: Rank Your Worries

Pick the least anxiety-provoking item on your list of worries and write it at the top of a new list. Then put down the next least distressing worry. Continue until you have ordered all of your worries, ranking them into a hierarchy that runs from the least to the most anxiety provoking. Here's an example of a hierarchy composed by Rachel.

1. *Forgetting to send my sister a birthday card.*

2. *Driving on the school field trip and losing my way.*

3. *Forgetting to pick up Cathy after school.*

4. *Missing a doctor's appointment.*

5. *Missing the property tax deadline.*

6. *Making a mistake at work and getting audited.*

3: Relax

You are ready to work with the first worry on your list. Get into a comfortable position, breathe deeply, and do cue-controlled relaxation. Let any tension drain out of your body.

4: Visualize a Worry

Vividly imagine the first (easiest) item from your hierarchy of worries. See this situation occurring over and over again. Stick with the worst possible outcome of that situation and focus on the sights, sounds, tastes, scents, and sensations as if the event were really happening to you. Using all five senses makes your scene much more vivid. Don't just see the scene from an outside vantage point, as if you were watching a movie. Rather, imagine that you are an active participant, in the middle of the action.

Try not to imagine any alternative scenarios. Stick with the worst possible outcome. Don't allow your mind to wander and escape into distraction. Do this for twenty-five minutes. Set a kitchen timer to keep track of the time. Don't stop early, even if your anxiety is high, or even if you're bored.

Rachel imagined getting a phone call from her sister Mary. She heard Mary's ring tone and saw her hand reach for her cell phone, felt the slick glass of the phone as she answered and held it to her ear. Her sister's voice said, "Well hi, stranger," just as Rachel realized with horror that Mary's birthday was last week and she had forgotten. She focused on the shame and embarrassment, imagining Mary sarcastically saying, "So, you've been busy, or you just don't love me anymore?" Rachel imagined this outcome for twenty-five minutes, going over the scene to add enriching details. She resisted engaging with alternative scenarios until the time was up.

If you try this approach and find that your anxiety is low, nowhere near the level you feel during a "real" worry session, you may be having trouble creating sufficiently vivid images. Try switching to different senses. Most people imagine with visual images, but some do better with sounds, textures, or scents.

For example, John couldn't feel really anxious using visual images of being in a car wreck. Then he switched to other senses and imagined the sounds of screeching tires, metal smashing, glass breaking, and sirens. He imagined the texture of asphalt and broken glass, and the smell of leaking gasoline, blood, and smoke. These sensory images worked so well that he rated his anxiety at 95 out of a 100.

5: Rate Your Peak Anxiety

While you're visualizing, rate your highest anxiety level. You can jot down numbers on a piece of scrap paper without even opening your eyes. Use a rating of 0 for no anxiety and a rating of 100 for the worst anxiety you've ever experienced. Rachel gave her scene a 70 after the first five minutes. But later in the scene, she really frightened herself and raised the rating to a 90.

6: Imagine Alternatives

After a full twenty-five minutes of visualizing the worst possible outcome, allow yourself to visualize alternative, less stressful outcomes. Don't start early, and once you do start, spend just five minutes imagining an outcome that isn't as bad as your worst-case scenario.

After her shame and horror, Rachel imagined that she had initiated the call, and that she called just one day after her sister's birthday. She imagined apologizing and saying that a belated gift was in the mail.

7: Rate Your Anxiety Again

After five minutes of imagining alternative outcomes, rate your anxiety again. It will probably be notably lower than your previous rating. Rachel rated her final scene at 30.

8: Repeat Steps 4 through 7

Continue working with the same worry, repeating steps 4 through 7 until your peak anxiety when imagining the worst possible outcome is 25 or less.

Then do these same steps for the next worry on your hierarchy. Do at least one session each day. If you have time and can tolerate it, you can do several sessions a day. By the time you've worked through your hierarchy, you should find that your worry is significantly reduced.

It took Rachel four weeks to work through her hierarchy, averaging one-and-a-half sessions a day. During that period, she worried a lot less. Whenever she started to worry, she told herself that she could postpone the worry until her next scheduled session. Even after she stopped doing regular worry exposure, Rachel found that her fear of making mistakes and forgetting things was significantly reduced. She would start to worry, remember her exposure sessions, and think, "I've worried this into the ground already." She was usually able to stop worrying soon, or at least switch to a more balanced assessment of alternative outcomes.

Worry Behavior Prevention

You may habitually perform or avoid certain behaviors to keep bad things from happening. For example, Pete never read the obituaries or drove past the cemetery, feeling that his avoidance would somehow keep loved ones from dying. His mother always knocked on wood whenever she made a positive prediction.

However, such ritual or preventive behaviors actually perpetuate worry and have no power to prevent bad things from happening. For Pete, active avoidance of the obituaries and the cemetery just made him worry about death more often, and he knew intellectually that such avoidance couldn't actually keep people from dying.

The good news is, stopping these behaviors is a relatively straightforward process that involves five simple steps:

1. Record your worry behavior.

2. Pick the easiest behavior to stop and predict the consequences of stopping it.

3. Stop the easiest behavior or replace it with a new behavior.

4. Assess your anxiety before and after.

5. Repeat steps 2 through 4 with the next-easiest behavior.

1: Record Your Behavior

In your journal, write down the things you do or avoid doing to prevent the disasters you worry about from happening.

Here's an example from Carly, who was very worried about social disapproval. She couldn't stand the thought that others might think she was impolite, a bad hostess, or not doing her fair share. She identified three worry behaviors:

Getting to appointments and parties too early, and then driving around the block for twenty minutes until it's time to go in.

Taking a main dish, a salad, and a dessert to potlucks, instead of just one dish, as expected.

Making way too much food for parties.

2: Identify Consequences

Pick the worry behavior that would be easiest to stop and write it down. Then write down the predicted consequences.

Carly picked making too much food for her parties. She predicted simply: "We'd run out of food halfway through the party."

3: Stop or Replace a Behavior

This is the hard part. In order to find out if your prediction will come true, you have to be a good scientist and actually run the experiment. Resolve to refrain from the behavior the next time you start worrying.

Carly firmly decided that she would not make too much food for her son's birthday party. Unfortunately, she couldn't just stop the worry behavior entirely—she had to make *some* food. She carefully figured out how much food the average party guest ate and how many guests were coming, and then prepared just enough food based on those calculations. Every time she felt the temptation to add a fudge factor, she stifled it.

If your worry behavior is a form of avoidance, such as not driving past the cemetery or never reading obituaries, you need to take a different approach: You have to start doing what you've been avoiding. Resolve to drive past the cemetery every morning on the way to work or to read obituaries with your morning coffee.

Sometimes even the seemingly easiest behavior to stop isn't so easy. In that case, create a hierarchy of replacement behaviors that allows you to taper off from your worry behavior.

Stan was a perfectionistic legal secretary who worried about making mistakes on the senior partner's contracts and briefs. He would take an important brief home and spend hours of his own time proofing and reproofing it, agonizing over possible typos, and changing type sizes and fonts far into the night. Every time he made the slightest alteration, he would run the entire document through the spell-checker again.

The thought of spell-checking and proofing just once and declaring a brief done was too alarming for Stan to even consider. So he made up this hierarchy and resolved to start with the first (easiest) item on his list that day.

- *Take brief home and do three extra passes through it.*

- *Take brief home and do two extra passes.*

- *Take brief home and do one extra pass.*

- *Stay up to one hour late and leave brief at work with no extra pass.*

- *Leave brief at work and go home on time. No extra pass.*

- *Deliberately leave one punctuation error in brief.*

- *Deliberately leave one grammatical error.*

- *Deliberately leave one spelling error.*

Stan worked through each step of this hierarchy. For each, he predicted dire consequences and experienced high anxiety. At each step, however, those consequences failed to occur, so he gained confidence for the next step.

You'll notice that the last three steps involve making deliberate mistakes. This is a good strategy to extinguish checking behaviors designed to prevent mistakes. Stan found that making small mistakes didn't cause the firm to lose cases, and also didn't get him fired. Nobody even noticed the errors. He was eventually able to eliminate other checking behaviors and reduce his perfectionism to what he called "high but not inflexible standards."

4: Assess Before and After

When you felt like performing your old behavior and knew you weren't going to do it, how anxious were you? Rate your anxiety on a scale of 0 to 100, where 0 means no anxiety.

Then assess how anxious you felt after performing your new behavior or cutting out your old behavior, using the same scale. Did your anxiety diminish?

Carly, the woman who habitually prepared too much food for guests, rated her anxiety a full 100 just before her son's birthday party. She was gratified to find it had reduced to just 25 by the end of the party, when there was still a little food left and the party had been a success.

Also be sure to observe the actual consequences. What actually happened as a result of your behavioral change? Did your dire predictions come true?

In Carly's case, her prediction didn't come true; she didn't run out of food halfway through the party. She felt more confidence about her ability to enter into a social engagement without excessive worry and preventive behavior.

5: The Next-Easiest Behavior

From your initial list, pick the worry behavior that is the next-easiest to stop and repeat steps 2 through 4: Predict the consequences of stopping the behavior. Then stop it and replace it with a new behavior if appropriate. Finally, assess your anxiety level before and after the experiment.

Example: Rhonda

Rhonda's experience with worry control shows how all four steps fit together. She was chronically worried about being rejected by her boyfriend, her boss, her parents, and complete strangers. She avoided meeting new people for fear that they would reject her. She kept checking with her boyfriend, Josh, to make sure he still loved her. She would say, "I love you," to him in such a way that he had to respond, "I love you too." Some evenings she'd do this five or six times, until it started to annoy Josh, who complained about her neediness.

Rhonda learned progressive muscle relaxation and did it every evening after dinner or just before she went to bed. She also mastered cue-controlled relaxation and set her watch alarm so every three hours she would remember to stop, take a few deep breaths, and relax. This helped reduce her ongoing arousal level so the chronic worries in the back of her mind didn't build as much throughout the day.

Rhonda worked on her Risk Assessment Worksheet while she was learning relaxation skills. When she assessed the risk of Josh dumping her, she realized two things: first, that the odds were greatly against him dumping her;

and second, if he did dump her, she could survive the rejection and cope with the loneliness. She found it very interesting and instructive to see how persistent overestimation and catastrophizing had been feeding her worry.

Next, Rhonda made a hierarchy of rejection experiences to use in worry exposure. She started with the mild rejection experience of being asked by a bus driver to step to the rear of the bus. After only two sessions, that scene elicited only minor anxiety, so she went on to extinguish her reaction to scenes involving her boss asking her to redo sloppy work, her mom rejecting her ideas for the family reunion, and, finally, Josh saying he wanted to break up.

She concluded worry control treatment with two kinds of worry behavior prevention. She prevented her avoidance of strangers by forcing herself to say something to whoever sat next to her on the bus each morning. She learned that some people responded and some didn't—and that she survived both types of responses. To change her checking behavior with Josh, she resolved to say, "I love you," only twice a day. Then she cut it down to once a day. Then she said it every other day. Interestingly, the less she said, "I love you," to Josh, the more he said it to her without prompting.

~

It will take you one or two weeks to learn to relax using deep breathing, cue-controlled relaxation, and visualization. During this time, you can also begin the process of assessing risks. Then you can begin to conduct worry exposure. You should notice improvements by your second or third exposure session.

Worry prevention takes only an hour or two to put into practice, and its benefits can be felt immediately. All told, you can expect to see progress in about a month.

Chapter 6

GETTING

MOBILIZED

One of the effects of depression is feeling immobilized. It's hard to push yourself to do normal self-care activities, and pleasure seems all but absent from your life. Feeling immobilized is not only a symptom of depression; it is also a cause. The less you do, the more depressed you feel, and the more depressed you feel, the less you do. It's a downward spiral that maintains withdrawal from life and prolongs depression.

The solution is to push yourself to higher levels of activity even though you don't feel like it.

Activity Scheduling

A technique known as *activity scheduling* can reenergize you and offer significant help in overcoming depression.

In this technique, you focus on adding two different types of activities to your schedule: activities that are pleasurable, and activities that give you a sense of mastery. These categories aren't mutually exclusive; some activities may give you a sense of both pleasure and mastery. This chapter explains activity scheduling in detail and will help you implement the technique. Here's an overview of the process:

1. Record and rate activities

2. Schedule new activities

3. Select new activities

4. Predict pleasure or mastery levels

5. Compare actual levels to predictions

1: Record and Rate Activities

Download a copy of the Weekly Activity Schedule from http://www.newharbinger.com/48695 or use a blank page in your journal. Over the next week, record your main activity or activities during each hour. If you don't have time to record your activities during the day, be sure to record them no later than that evening.

You'll use the information in a few different ways: to assess which of your current activities give you a sense of pleasure or mastery; to find times when you can schedule additional pleasure or mastery activities; and to establish an activity baseline so you can recognize your progress. In the weeks ahead, you'll implement your plan to both mobilize yourself and help yourself feel less depressed.

When monitoring and recording activities during this first week, pay attention to two aspects of your experience: pleasure and mastery. If an activity has provided you any pleasure at all, write the letter P in that box and rate how pleasurable the activity was on a scale from 1 (minimal pleasure) to 10 (extreme pleasure).

Also identify mastery activities, in which you take care of yourself or others. Tasks you may have been avoiding, like answering a letter, weeding your garden, preparing a healthful meal, or running an errand, are particularly good choices for mastery items. (A list of typical mastery activities appears in step 3.) If an activity gave you a sense of mastery, write the letter M in that box and rate your sense of mastery, *given how tired or depressed you may have felt at the time.* Again, use a scale from 1 (minimal sense of mastery) to 10 (extreme sense of mastery).

Don't rate how much you objectively achieved or what you think you would have achieved before you were depressed. Rather, assess your sense of mastery taking into account how hard this activity was in light of how you were feeling.

Identifying and rating pleasure and mastery activities can help you recognize how your life has gotten out of balance, that many things you formerly enjoyed are no longer part of your week, or that your current activities provide very little emotional nourishment.

Pleasure ratings also give you information about the activities you still enjoy and which ones offer the best boost to your mood. Noticing and rating mastery activities may help you recognize that, despite everything, you're still trying hard. You're still doing things to cope. And even though you may not be as efficient or effective as you were before you became depressed, the things you do are real achievements, given how you feel.

2: Schedule New Activities

Once you've filled out your Weekly Activity Schedule for the first week, use it to look for times when you can schedule additional pleasure and mastery activities during your week. Identify at least ten hours when you're engaged in an optional activity that provides neither pleasure nor a sense of mastery. See if you can find one or two hours each day when you can schedule new pleasure or mastery activities to replace old, unprofitable activities.

3: Select New Activities

Analyzing your pleasure and mastery ratings for the first week may give you some direction in scheduling new pleasure and mastery activities. However, you'll probably need to branch out beyond what you've been doing and identify new activities to try, or start engaging in former activities once again. If you've been depressed for a while, you may have a hard time coming up with ideas, so here's a list for inspiration. You may also get some ideas by consulting friends or family members. Pleasure activities can include:

- Visiting friends or family
- Talking on the phone
- Going to movies or plays

- Watching videos or TV

- Exercising

- Doing sports

- Playing games

- Doing computer activities

- Surfing the Internet

- Chatting on the Internet

- Listening to music

- Going away for a weekend

- Planning a vacation

- Pursuing a hobby

- Collecting

- Doing crafts

- Enjoying the sun

- Relaxing with a hot drink

- Listening to audio books

- Doing guided meditations

- Walking or hiking
- Shopping
- Taking a hot bath
- Reading
- Gardening
- Writing
- Going out to eat
- Eating a favorite treat
- Being held or touched
- Getting a massage
- Engaging in sexual activities
- Going for a drive
- Going on a picnic
- Sitting in a peaceful place
- Writing letters
- Engaging in artistic pursuits
- Watching or reading the news

This list includes just a few of the many possibilities for activities that might bring you pleasure. In your journal, write some of your ideas about activities that would be pleasurable for you. Think back over the years to the things you've enjoyed. Try to remember everything you've ever done that was fun. Review the list and identify specific new activities within those generic categories.

For instance, games you enjoy might be pool or cards. For crafts, you may enjoy needlepoint or building model airplanes. Artistic pursuits could mean going to galleries or writing haiku. When it comes to calling or visiting friends, there may be certain people you enjoy spending more time with. Take some time right now to write down specific activities that you have enjoyed or can imagine enjoying in the future.

Don't be surprised if you currently have a hard time doing this. Many of the things you've enjoyed in the past can seem like a hassle or a burden. This is due to depression. When you begin to include more pleasurable activities in your week you'll feel better, even if those activities seem uninteresting now. Right now, select five to seven pleasure activities from your list to schedule for the next week.

You also need to add new mastery activities. Often these are self-care activities you may have neglected. You may need to shop for groceries, run errands, clean or straighten up around the house, write letters, or make important calls. When you're depressed and immobilized, even these normal daily tasks can seem impossibly hard. Here's a list of some typical mastery activities you might schedule into your week.

- Shopping

- Going to the bank

- Helping children with homework

- Supervising children's bedtime

- Bathing

- Preparing a hot meal

- Paying bills

- Getting up before 9:00 a.m.

- Walking the dog

- Fixing something
- Cleaning something
- Doing dishes
- Exercising or stretching
- Resolving a conflict
- Doing laundry
- Gardening
- Running an errand
- Tackling challenging tasks at work
- Folding and putting away clothes
- Solving a problem
- Straightening up the house
- Decorating
- Doing car maintenance
- Making a business call
- Returning telephone calls
- Writing in a journal

- Doing self-help exercises

- Engaging in spiritual or religious activities

- Grooming

- Getting a haircut

- Dressing up

- Writing letters

- Arranging activities for your children

- Engaging in artistic pursuits

- Driving your children to activities

- Going to work

As with pleasure activities, these are just a few; most are fairly generic. After reviewing the list, make your own list of specific activities that might give you a sense of mastery or accomplishment. Take some time right now to fill in all of the blanks below with mastery activities that you might schedule into your week.

Right now, select five to seven mastery activities to sprinkle throughout the coming week, with a particular focus on tasks you may have been avoiding. If you've been putting off doing the recycling, make an appointment with yourself on your Weekly Activity Schedule to get it done. If you've been putting off renewing your driver's license, write in a definite time when you'll accomplish this task.

However, don't try to do more than one extra mastery activity each day; that may be pushing too hard and leave you feeling overwhelmed.

In your Weekly Activity Schedule from the first week, look for times when you've been unproductive and had neither pleasure nor a sense of mastery. These are ideal times to substitute a mastery activity that can give you a sense of achievement.

Note that some mastery activities may be too involved to accomplish in an hour or too overwhelming when tackled all at once. In such cases, it may help to break the activity into smaller steps that you can accomplish in fifteen minutes or less. For example, a plan to improve the appearance of your living room might involve many steps, starting with a decision to buy and hang a new poster. Some mastery activities may stretch over two or more weeks as you work through each step in the process.

We encourage you to make your commitment to pleasure activities as important as your commitment to mastery activities. Increasing the number of enjoyable experiences in your week is an essential step to overcoming depression and getting your life back in balance.

4: Predict Pleasure or Mastery Levels

An important part of planning new activities is trying to anticipate how they will make you feel. Now that you've filled out a new Weekly Activity Schedule for the coming week, take some time right now to predict how much of a sense of pleasure or mastery you'll get from each activity. Use the same scale of P1 to P10 for pleasure activities and M1 to M10 for mastery activities, where 10 indicates extreme pleasure or mastery, and then circle your ratings.

Most depressed people make very conservative predictions about the amount of pleasure or achievement they'll feel during a planned activity. It's okay to not feel hopeful. You may anticipate very little in the way of good feelings from your planned activities. But do them anyway and evaluate what happens.

5: Compare Actual Levels to Predictions

During the week, write your actual pleasure or mastery rating for each new activity next to your circled prediction. You're likely to find that your actual ratings are higher than your predictions. Because depression tends to make you pessimistic, comparing your prediction to the actual level of pleasure or mastery you experience may help you recognize how depression distorts your view of things. The fact that your new activities are more enjoyable and fulfilling than you anticipated could help you resist the discouraging inner voice that tells you, "Don't bother with anything new; it's a lot of work, and you'll still feel lousy."

Additional Tips

Some people feel they don't have time in their week for anything new. Because the Weekly Activity Schedule is a crucial intervention for overcoming depression, you may need to limit or suspend some of your usual activities so you can work in more pleasure and mastery experiences. Go through your first Weekly Activity Schedule and cross out any box where the activity isn't absolutely essential. These are the hours when you can substitute new pleasure and mastery activities.

After four or five weeks of adding new activities, you're likely to find that your days are becoming rather full. At this point a certain amount of pruning may be in order to eliminate some of the new activities that offer little nourishment. At this stage, you can also cut down on the number of new activities you add each week. However, still continue to make plans on your Weekly Activity Schedule. Writing activities down increases the chance that you'll do them. Keep filling in planned mastery and pleasure activities in your weekly schedule until you feel a significant improvement in your level of depression.

The first step in this process is monitoring and recording your activities for one week. After that, you will take four to eight weeks to schedule and gradually increase specific types of activities. You may begin to see some benefits as soon as you start engaging in newly scheduled activities.

CONCLUSION

Each of the techniques in this book is designed to change the way you habitually react to things. However, your old ways of reacting have been with you a long time. They're familiar and therefore difficult to change. Old habits are hard to part with, even when they clearly contribute to your pain.

CBT isn't a "talking cure" like traditional psychoanalysis. In this approach, change doesn't arise from a series of insights gained during analysis, conversation, rumination, or merely reading about your problem. It happens because you do something. You must diligently practice the various exercises in this book. Here are strategies to overcome common difficulties along the way.

Strengthen Your Imagination

A common roadblock is an untrained imagination. To strengthen your imagination, reread the Visualization Skills section in chapter 4.

Cultivate Belief

Another major obstacle is simply not believing that a technique or exercise will work. Failure to believe is a cognitive problem. You repeat discouraging statements to yourself, such as "I'll never get better," "This won't work," "These sorts of things don't help me," "I'm too stupid," or "Somebody has to show me how."

One of the basic tenets of this book is that you believe what you repeat to yourself. If you say any negative statement often enough, you'll act in such a way as to make it true for you.

This book will be of little or no value until you overcome the belief that it cannot help you. To work on this issue, commit to a specific period of focused effort: two weeks, one week, even one day. Then evaluate any change in your problem at that time. If you've made a little progress, if the symptom is less painful or frequent, commit to continuing your work with the book for a second period of time.

Choose Boredom

Many of these techniques are boring. But they work. Practicing them becomes a trade-off: a few weeks of occasional boredom in exchange for years of freedom from unwanted symptoms. This is the choice you may have to make every day when you do these exercises.

Be an Active Creator

Fear of novelty is a well-documented obstacle to successful treatment. Your worldview changes when you realize that you have the power to change how you think and therefore how you feel.

When you give up a symptom, your life changes. Many people would rather hold on to a familiar though painful symptom than adjust to a new life without it. You can no longer see yourself as a helpless victim of good and bad fortune; *you are an active creator of your own experience.*

Adjust Directions

Just following new directions may provoke anxiety. The directions may not quite fit your needs. They may be too detailed, cumbersome, or rigid. They may be insufficiently detailed. Either way, bear in mind that the directions are intended to provide a general outline; adjust them to fit your individual needs.

Schedule Priorities

Poor time management is a major roadblock to success. People who give up after half learning a technique often explain that they were overscheduled and didn't have time to use the technique. Here the real problem is usually one of priorities. Other things simply had a higher priority. After-work drinks, errands, long phone calls, television, or surfing the Internet came first. You need to schedule your work with this book just as you do other important parts of your day. Write down the time and place and keep the commitment just as you would an appointment with a friend.

Continue Using Techniques

Another difficulty, often overlooked, is success that comes too rapidly. In this case, there's a danger that you may think, "That was a snap to get over. Maybe it wasn't a problem after all. I don't have to worry about that anymore." Minimizing a symptom's significance in this way lays the groundwork for a setback. The symptom may gradually reemerge in your patterns of behavior, perhaps without your immediate awareness. To avoid this, continue using the techniques you've learned in this book for a while after you're free of symptoms. If symptoms do reoccur, immediately revisit the relevant chapters and work through them again.

If you find yourself skipping practice sessions or just going through the motions halfheartedly, ask yourself these questions:

- Why am I doing these exercises?

- Are they really important to me?

- What am I doing or what would I like to be doing instead of these exercises?

- Is this alternative activity more important to me than doing the exercises?

- Can I schedule my life so I can do both?

- If I don't do the exercises now, exactly when and where will I do them next?

- What would I have to give up if I succeeded with my exercises?

- What would I have to confront if I succeeded with my exercises?

Persist. Don't give up. Your ability to heal yourself by modifying your thoughts and feelings is a tremendous power. You can change what you think and therefore what you feel.

You can change the structure of your life by altering the structure of your mind.

You can take away your pain.

RESOURCES

You may also find these resources from New Harbinger Publications helpful.

Activating Happiness, Rachel Hershenberg, 2017.

The Anxiety and Phobia Workbook, Edmund J. Bourne, 2020 (7th edition).

Anxiety Happens, John P. Forsyth and Georg H. Eifert, 2018.

The Anxious Thoughts Workbook, David A. Clark, 2018.

The Cognitive Behavioral Workbook for Anxiety, William J. Knaus, 2014 (2nd edition).

The Cognitive Behavioral Workbook for Depression, William J. Knaus and Albert Ellis, 2012 (2nd edition).

The Mindfulness and Acceptance Workbook for Anxiety, John P. Forsyth and Georg H. Eifert, 2016 (2nd edition).

The Mindfulness and Acceptance Workbook for Depression, Kirk D. Strosahl and Patricia J. Robinson, 2017 (2nd edition).

Needing to Know for Sure, Martin N. Seif and Sally M. Winston, 2019.

The Negative Thoughts Workbook, David A. Clark, 2020.

Perfectly Hidden Depression, Margaret Robinson Rutherford, 2019.

The Relaxation and Stress Reduction Workbook, Martha Davis, Elizabeth Robbins Eshelman, and Matthew McKay, 2019 (7th edition).

Thoughts and Feelings, Matthew McKay, Martha Davis, and Patrick Fanning, 2021 (5th edition).

The Upward Spiral, Alex Korb, 2015.

The Upward Spiral Workbook, Alex Korb, 2019.

The Upward Spiral Card Deck, Alex Korb, 2020.

Matthew McKay, PhD, is a professor at the Wright Institute in Berkeley, CA. He has authored and coauthored numerous books, including *Self-Esteem, The Relaxation and Stress Reduction Workbook, Thoughts and Feelings,* and *ACT on Life Not on Anger.* His books combined have sold more than four million copies. He received his PhD in clinical psychology from the California School of Professional Psychology, and specializes in the cognitive behavioral treatment of anxiety and depression.

Martha Davis, PhD, was a psychologist in the department of psychiatry at Kaiser Permanente Medical Center in Santa Clara, CA; where she practiced individual, couples, and group psychotherapy for almost thirty years prior to her retirement. She is coauthor of *Thoughts and Feelings, The Relaxation and Stress Reduction Workbook,* and *Messages.*

Patrick Fanning is a professional writer in the mental health field, and founder of a men's support group in Northern California. He has authored and coauthored twelve self-help books, including *Self-Esteem, Thoughts and Feelings, Couple Skills,* and *Mind and Emotions.*

Real change *is* possible

For more than forty-five years, New Harbinger has published proven-effective self-help books and pioneering workbooks to help readers of all ages and backgrounds improve mental health and well-being, and achieve lasting personal growth. In addition, our spirituality books offer profound guidance for deepening awareness and cultivating healing, self-discovery, and fulfillment.

Founded by psychologist Matthew McKay and Patrick Fanning, New Harbinger is proud to be an independent, employee-owned company. Our books reflect our core values of integrity, innovation, commitment, sustainability, compassion, and trust. Written by leaders in the field and recommended by therapists worldwide, New Harbinger books are practical, accessible, and provide real tools for real change.

 new**harbinger**publications

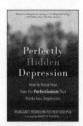

Did you know there are **free tools** you can download for this book?

Free tools are things like **worksheets, guided meditation exercises**, and **more** that will help you get the most out of your book.

You can download free tools for this book—whether you bought or borrowed it, in any format, from any source—from the New Harbinger website. All you need is a NewHarbinger.com account. Just use the URL provided in this book to view the free tools that are available for it. Then, click on the "download" button for the free tool you want, and follow the prompts that appear to log in to your NewHarbinger.com account and download the material.

You can also save the free tools for this book to your **Free Tools Library** so you can access them again anytime, just by logging in to your account! Just look for this button on the book's free tools page.

+ Save this to my free tools library